GRATITUDE
JOURNAL

Interrupt Anxiety With Gratitude

This Journal belongs to

_____

ISBN: 978-1-952358-13-5

Gratitude

Gratitude is a feeling of appreciation for what one has. It is a feeling of thankfulness for the blessings we have received. Feeling gratitude in the present moment makes you happier and more relaxed, and improves your overall health and well-being.

Affirmations are words that we consciously choose to say. When we repeat affirmations, they get imprinted in the subconscious mind. Therefore, it is key that we use positive affirmations if we want to create a positive life for ourselves.

There is an exercise at the beginning of this journal to complete before starting your daily record of gratitude and affirmation.

By keeping a record of your gratitude in a journal, you will store positive energy, gain clarity in your life, and have greater control of your thoughts and emotions.

Each day, write down three to five things that you are grateful for in this journal and turn your ordinary moments into blessings.

A gentle word, a kind look, a good-natured smile can work wonders and accomplish miracles. ~ *William Hazlitt*

People I am *Grateful* for:

_____

_____

_____

_____

_____

_____

_____

_____

Top 10 memorable events in my life that
I am *Grateful* for:

1. _____

2. _____

3. _____

4. _____

5. _____

6. _____

7. _____

8. _____

9. _____

10. _____

People I have made a difference to and am *Grateful* for having had this opportunity:

_____

_____

_____

_____

_____

_____

_____

Top 10 places I have visited and am *Grateful* for:

1. _____

2. _____

3. _____

4. _____

5. _____

6. _____

7. _____

8. _____

9. _____

10. _____

The times when I have laughed so hard that I cried and which I am now *Grateful* for:

_____

_____

_____

_____

_____

_____

_____

Top 10 things that I was scared to do but am now *Grateful* for having done:

1. _____

2. _____

3. _____

4. _____

5. _____

6. _____

7. _____

8. _____

9. _____

10. _____

Things I have now which I am *Grateful* for:

_____

_____

_____

_____

_____

_____

_____

Top 10 teachable moments from my past
that I am now *Grateful* for:

1. _____

2. _____

3. _____

4. _____

5. _____

6. _____

7. _____

8. _____

9. _____

10. _____

Something that I am looking forward to:

_____

_____

_____

_____

_____

_____

Top 10 things I'd like to accomplish:

1. _____

2. _____

3. _____

4. _____

5. _____

6. _____

7. _____

8. _____

9. _____

10. _____

Day: _____ *Date:* ____ / ____ / ____

Today I am *Grateful* for _____

_____

_____

_____

_____

_____

Today's Affirmation _____

Courtesies of a small and trivial character are the ones which strike deepest in
the grateful and appreciating heart. ~ *Henry Clay*

Day: _____ *Date:* ____ / ____ / ____

Today I am *Grateful* for _____

_____

_____

_____

_____

_____

Today's Affirmation _____

Day: _____ *Date:* ____/____/____

Today I am *Grateful* for _____

_____

_____

_____

_____

Today's Affirmation _____

Being deeply loved by someone gives you strength, while loving someone
deeply gives you courage. ~ *Lao Tzu*

Day: _____ *Date:* ____/____/____

Today I am *Grateful* for _____

_____

_____

_____

_____

Today's Affirmation _____

Day: _____ *Date:* ____ / ____ / ____

Today I am *Grateful* for _____

_____

_____

_____

_____

Today's Affirmation _____

The most certain sign of wisdom is cheerfulness. ~ *Michel de Montaigne*

Day: _____ *Date:* ____ / ____ / ____

Today I am *Grateful* for _____

_____

_____

_____

_____

Today's Affirmation _____

Day: _____ *Date:* ____/ ____/ ____

Today I am *Grateful* for _____

_____

_____

_____

_____

Today's Affirmation _____

Keep love in your heart. A life without it is like a sunless garden when the
flowers are dead. ~ *Oscar Wilde*

Day: _____ *Date:* ____/ ____/ ____

Today I am *Grateful* for _____

_____

_____

_____

_____

Today's Affirmation _____

11

Day: _____ *Date:* ____ / ____ / ____

Today I am *Grateful* for _____

_____

_____

_____

_____

_____

Today's Affirmation _____

Let us be grateful to people who make us happy, they are the charming
gardeners who make our souls blossom. ~ *Marcel Proust*

Day: _____ *Date:* ____ / ____ / ____

Today I am *Grateful* for _____

_____

_____

_____

_____

_____

Today's Affirmation _____

Day: _____ *Date:* ___ / ___ / ___

Today I am *Grateful* for _____

_____

_____

_____

_____

Today's Affirmation _____

The thankful receiver bears a plentiful harvest. ~ *William Blake*

Day: _____ *Date:* ___ / ___ / ___

Today I am *Grateful* for _____

_____

_____

_____

_____

Today's Affirmation _____

Day: _____ *Date:* ____ / ____ / ____

Today I am *Grateful* for _____

_____

_____

_____

_____

_____

Today's Affirmation _____

Our greatest glory is not in never falling, but in rising every time we fall.
~ *Confucius*

Day: _____ *Date:* ____ / ____ / ____

Today I am *Grateful* for _____

_____

_____

_____

_____

_____

Today's Affirmation _____

Day: _____ *Date:* ____/____/____

Today I am *Grateful* for _____

_____

_____

_____

_____

_____

Today's Affirmation _____

Happiness is not an ideal of reason, but of imagination. ~ *Immanuel Kant*

Day: _____ *Date:* ____/____/____

Today I am *Grateful* for _____

_____

_____

_____

_____

_____

Today's Affirmation _____

Day: _____ *Date:* ____ / ____ / ____

Today I am *Grateful* for _____

_____

_____

_____

_____

Today's Affirmation _____

The art of being happy lies in the power of extracting happiness from
common things. ~ *Henry Ward Beecher*

Day: _____ *Date:* ____ / ____ / ____

Today I am *Grateful* for _____

_____

_____

_____

_____

Today's Affirmation _____

Day: _____ *Date:* ____/____/____

Today I am *Grateful* for _____

_____

_____

_____

_____

_____

Today's Affirmation _____

The clearest way into the Universe is through a forest wilderness.
~ *John Muir*

Day: _____ *Date:* ____/____/____

Today I am *Grateful* for _____

_____

_____

_____

_____

_____

Today's Affirmation _____

Day: _____ *Date:* ____ / ____ / ____

Today I am *Grateful* for _____

_____

_____

_____

_____

_____

Today's Affirmation _____

Gratitude is a state of being and should be directed towards everything that
you are creating in this life.

Day: _____ *Date:* ____ / ____ / ____

Today I am *Grateful* for _____

_____

_____

_____

_____

_____

Today's Affirmation _____

Day: _____ *Date:* ____ / ____ / ____

Today I am *Grateful* for _____

_____

_____

_____

_____

_____

Today's Affirmation _____

The pleasure which we most rarely experience gives us greatest delight.
~ *Epictetus*

Day: _____ *Date:* ____ / ____ / ____

Today I am *Grateful* for _____

_____

_____

_____

_____

_____

Today's Affirmation _____

Day: _____ *Date:* ____ / ____ / ____

Today I am *Grateful* for _____

_____

_____

_____

_____

Today's Affirmation _____

Our happiness depends on wisdom all the way. ~ *Sophocles*

Day: _____ *Date:* ____ / ____ / ____

Today I am *Grateful* for _____

_____

_____

_____

_____

Today's Affirmation _____

Day: _____ *Date:* ____/ ____/ ____

Today I am *Grateful* for _____

_____

_____

_____

_____

Today's Affirmation _____

To live is so startling it leaves little time for anything else.
~ *Emily Dickinson*

Day: _____ *Date:* ____/ ____/ ____

Today I am *Grateful* for _____

_____

_____

_____

_____

Today's Affirmation _____

Day: _____ *Date:* ____ / ____ / ____

Today I am *Grateful* for _____

_____

_____

_____

_____

Today's Affirmation _____

Happiness resides not in possessions, and not in gold, happiness dwells
in the soul. ~ *Democritus*

Day: _____ *Date:* ____ / ____ / ____

Today I am *Grateful* for _____

_____

_____

_____

_____

Today's Affirmation _____

Day: _____ *Date:* ____ / ____ / ____

Today I am *Grateful* for _____

_____

_____

_____

_____

Today's Affirmation _____

The essence of all beautiful art, all great art, is gratitude.
~ *Friedrich Nietzsche*

Day: _____ *Date:* ____ / ____ / ____

Today I am *Grateful* for _____

_____

_____

_____

_____

Today's Affirmation _____

Day: _____ *Date:* ____ / ____ / ____

Today I am *Grateful* for _____

_____

_____

_____

_____

Today's Affirmation _____

A single grateful thought toward heaven is the most perfect prayer.
~ *Gotthold Ephraim Lessing*

Day: _____ *Date:* ____ / ____ / ____

Today I am *Grateful* for _____

_____

_____

_____

_____

Today's Affirmation _____

Day: _____ *Date:* ____ / ____ / ____

Today I am *Grateful* for _____

_____

_____

_____

_____

Today's Affirmation _____

The way to know life is to love many things. ~ *Vincent Van Gogh*

Day: _____ *Date:* ____ / ____ / ____

Today I am *Grateful* for _____

_____

_____

_____

_____

Today's Affirmation _____

Day: _____ *Date:* ____ / ____ / ____

Today I am *Grateful* for _____

_____

_____

_____

_____

Today's Affirmation _____

Gratitude is not only the greatest of virtues, but the parent of all the others.
~ *Marcus Tullius Cicero*

Day: _____ *Date:* ____ / ____ / ____

Today I am *Grateful* for _____

_____

_____

_____

_____

Today's Affirmation _____

Day: _____ *Date:* ____/ ____/ ____

Today I am *Grateful* for _____

_____

_____

_____

_____

Today's Affirmation _____

Gratitude is the sign of noble souls. ~ *Aesop Fables*

Day: _____ *Date:* ____/ ____/ ____

Today I am *Grateful* for _____

_____

_____

_____

_____

Today's Affirmation _____

Day: _____ *Date:* ____ / ____ / ____

Today I am *Grateful* for _____

_____

_____

_____

_____

Today's Affirmation _____

There is only one way to happiness and that is to cease worrying about things
which are beyond the power of our will. ~ *Epictetus*

Day: _____ *Date:* ____ / ____ / ____

Today I am *Grateful* for _____

_____

_____

_____

_____

Today's Affirmation _____

Day: _____ *Date:* ____ / ____ / ____

Today I am *Grateful* for _____

_____

_____

_____

_____

Today's Affirmation _____

Everything has beauty, but not everyone sees it. ~ *Confucius*

Day: _____ *Date:* ____ / ____ / ____

Today I am *Grateful* for _____

_____

_____

_____

_____

Today's Affirmation _____

Day: _____ *Date:* ____ / ____ / ____

Today I am *Grateful* for _____

_____

_____

_____

_____

_____

Today's Affirmation _____

This world is but a canvas to our imagination. ~ *Henry David Thoreau*

Day: _____ *Date:* ____ / ____ / ____

Today I am *Grateful* for _____

_____

_____

_____

_____

Today's Affirmation _____

Day: _____ *Date:* ____ / ____ / ____

Today I am *Grateful* for _____

_____

_____

_____

_____

Today's Affirmation _____

Real happiness is cheap enough, yet how dearly we pay for its counterfeit.
~ *Hosea Ballou*

Day: _____ *Date:* ____ / ____ / ____

Today I am *Grateful* for _____

_____

_____

_____

_____

Today's Affirmation _____

Day: _____ *Date:* ____ / ____ / ____

Today I am *Grateful* for _____

_____

_____

_____

_____

Today's Affirmation _____

> Never give up, for that is just the place and time that the tide will turn.
> ~ *Harriet Beecher Stowe*

Day: _____ *Date:* ____ / ____ / ____

Today I am *Grateful* for _____

_____

_____

_____

_____

Today's Affirmation _____

Day: _____ *Date:* ____ / ____ / ____

Today I am *Grateful* for _____

_____

_____

_____

_____

_____

Today's Affirmation _____

The power of imagination makes us infinite. ~ *John Muir*

Day: _____ *Date:* ____ / ____ / ____

Today I am *Grateful* for _____

_____

_____

_____

_____

Today's Affirmation _____

Day: _____ *Date:* ____ / ____ / ____

Today I am *Grateful* for _____

_____

_____

_____

_____

Today's Affirmation _____

Happiness is a choice that requires effort at times. ~ *Aeschylus*

Day: _____ *Date:* ____ / ____ / ____

Today I am *Grateful* for _____

_____

_____

_____

_____

Today's Affirmation _____

Day: _____ *Date:* ____ / ____ / ____

Today I am *Grateful* for _____

_____

_____

_____

_____

_____

Today's Affirmation _____

A contented mind is the greatest blessing a man can enjoy in this world.
~ *Joseph Addison*

Day: _____ *Date:* ____ / ____ / ____

Today I am *Grateful* for _____

_____

_____

_____

_____

_____

Today's Affirmation _____

Day: _____ *Date:* ____ / ____ / ____

Today I am *Grateful* for _____

_____

_____

_____

_____

_____

Today's Affirmation _____

What we obtain too cheap, we esteem too lightly; it is dearness only that
gives everything its value. ~ *Thomas Paine*

Day: _____ *Date:* ____ / ____ / ____

Today I am *Grateful* for _____

_____

_____

_____

_____

_____

Today's Affirmation _____

Day: _____ *Date:* ____/____/____

Today I am *Grateful* for _____

_____

_____

_____

_____

Today's Affirmation _____

Life in abundance comes only through great love. ~ *Elbert Hubbard*

Day: _____ *Date:* ____/____/____

Today I am *Grateful* for _____

_____

_____

_____

_____

Today's Affirmation _____

Day: _____ *Date:* ____ / ____ / ____

Today I am *Grateful* for _____

_____

_____

_____

_____

_____

Today's Affirmation _____

A loving heart is the beginning of all knowledge. ~ *Thomas Carlyle*

Day: _____ *Date:* ____ / ____ / ____

Today I am *Grateful* for _____

_____

_____

_____

_____

_____

Today's Affirmation _____

Day: _____ *Date:* ____ / ____ / ____

Today I am *Grateful* for _____

_____

_____

_____

_____

Today's Affirmation _____

There are two ways of spreading light: to be the candle or the mirror that reflects it. ~ *Edith Wharton*

Day: _____ *Date:* ____ / ____ / ____

Today I am *Grateful* for _____

_____

_____

_____

_____

Today's Affirmation _____

Day: _____ *Date:* ____ / ____ / ____

Today I am *Grateful* for _____

_____

_____

_____

_____

_____

Today's Affirmation _____

How very little can be done under the spirit of fear.
~ *Florence Nightingale*

Day: _____ *Date:* ____ / ____ / ____

Today I am *Grateful* for _____

_____

_____

_____

_____

_____

Today's Affirmation _____

Day: _____ *Date:* ____/ ____/ ____

Today I am *Grateful* for _____

_____

_____

_____

_____

_____

Today's Affirmation _____

Life is not a matter of holding good cards, but of playing a poor hand well.
~ *Robert Louis Stevenson*

Day: _____ *Date:* ____/ ____/ ____

Today I am *Grateful* for _____

_____

_____

_____

_____

Today's Affirmation _____

Day: _____ *Date:* ____ / ____ / ____

Today I am *Grateful* for _____

_____

_____

_____

_____

_____

Today's Affirmation _____

> Who knows, the mind has the key to all things besides.
> ~ *Amos Bronson Alcott*

Day: _____ *Date:* ____ / ____ / ____

Today I am *Grateful* for _____

_____

_____

_____

_____

Today's Affirmation _____

Day: _____ *Date:* ____ / ____ / ____

Today I am *Grateful* for _____

_____

_____

_____

_____

Today's Affirmation _____

The purpose creates the machine. ~ *Arthur Young*

Day: _____ *Date:* ____ / ____ / ____

Today I am *Grateful* for _____

_____

_____

_____

_____

Today's Affirmation _____

Day: _____ *Date:* _____ / _____ / _____

Today I am *Grateful* for _____

_____

_____

_____

_____

Today's Affirmation _____

Knowing is not enough; we must apply. Willing is not enough; we must do.
~ *Johann Wolfgang von Goethe*

Day: _____ *Date:* _____ / _____ / _____

Today I am *Grateful* for _____

_____

_____

_____

_____

Today's Affirmation _____

Day: _____ *Date:* ____/____/____

Today I am *Grateful* for _____

_____

_____

_____

_____

_____

Today's Affirmation _____

True originality consists not in a new manner but in a new vision.
~ *Edith Wharton*

Day: _____ *Date:* ____/____/____

Today I am *Grateful* for _____

_____

_____

_____

_____

_____

Today's Affirmation _____

Day: _____ *Date:* ____ / ____ / ____

Today I am *Grateful* for _____

_____

_____

_____

_____

Today's Affirmation _____

What is once well done is done forever.
~ *Henry David Thoreau*

Day: _____ *Date:* ____ / ____ / ____

Today I am *Grateful* for _____

_____

_____

_____

_____

Today's Affirmation _____

Day: _____ *Date:* ____ / ____ / ____

Today I am *Grateful* for _____

_____

_____

_____

_____

_____

Today's Affirmation _____

Live your life as though your every act were to become a universal law.
~ *Immanuel Kant*

Day: _____ *Date:* ____ / ____ / ____

Today I am *Grateful* for _____

_____

_____

_____

_____

_____

Today's Affirmation _____

Day: _____ *Date:* _____ / _____ / _____

Today I am *Grateful* for _____

_____

_____

_____

_____

Today's Affirmation _____

If you want the present to be different from the past, study the past.
~ *Baruch Spinoza*

Day: _____ *Date:* _____ / _____ / _____

Today I am *Grateful* for _____

_____

_____

_____

_____

Today's Affirmation _____

Day: _____ *Date:* ____ / ____ / ____

Today I am *Grateful* for _____

_____

_____

_____

_____

Today's Affirmation _____

The best preparation for tomorrow is to do today's work superbly well.
~ *William Osler*

Day: _____ *Date:* ____ / ____ / ____

Today I am *Grateful* for _____

_____

_____

_____

_____

Today's Affirmation _____

Day: _____ *Date:* ____ / ____ / ____

Today I am *Grateful* for _____

_____

_____

_____

_____

Today's Affirmation _____

Remember when life's path is steep to keep your mind even. ~ *Horace*

Day: _____ *Date:* ____ / ____ / ____

Today I am *Grateful* for _____

_____

_____

_____

_____

Today's Affirmation _____

Day: _____ *Date:* ____/____/____

Today I am *Grateful* for _____

_____

_____

_____

_____

_____

Today's Affirmation _____

Ask me not what I have, but what I am. ~ *Heinrich Heine*

Day: _____ *Date:* ____/____/____

Today I am *Grateful* for _____

_____

_____

_____

_____

Today's Affirmation _____

Day: _____ *Date:* ___ / ___ / ___

Today I am *Grateful* for _____

_____

_____

_____

_____

Today's Affirmation _____

> Great thoughts speak only to the thoughtful mind, but great actions
> speak to all mankind. ~ *Theodore Roosevelt*

Day: _____ *Date:* ___ / ___ / ___

Today I am *Grateful* for _____

_____

_____

_____

_____

Today's Affirmation _____

Day: _____ *Date:* ____ / ____ / ____

Today I am *Grateful* for _____

_____

_____

_____

_____

_____

Today's Affirmation _____

> To love oneself is the beginning of a lifelong romance.
> ~ *Oscar Wilde*

Day: _____ *Date:* ____ / ____ / ____

Today I am *Grateful* for _____

_____

_____

_____

_____

Today's Affirmation _____

Day: _____ *Date:* ___ / ___ / ___

Today I am *Grateful* for _____

_____

_____

_____

_____

_____

Today's Affirmation _____

It is our attitude at the beginning of a difficult task which, more than
anything else, will affect its successful outcome. ~ *William James*

Day: _____ *Date:* ___ / ___ / ___

Today I am *Grateful* for _____

_____

_____

_____

_____

_____

Today's Affirmation _____

Day: _____ *Date:* ____ / ____ / ____

Today I am *Grateful* for _____

_____

_____

_____

_____

_____

Today's Affirmation _____

Cheerfulness is the best promoter of health and is as friendly to the
mind as to the body. ~ *Joseph Addison*

Day: _____ *Date:* ____ / ____ / ____

Today I am *Grateful* for _____

_____

_____

_____

_____

Today's Affirmation _____

Day: _____ *Date:* ____ / ____ / ____

Today I am *Grateful* for _____

_____

_____

_____

_____

Today's Affirmation _____

It is costly wisdom that is bought by experience. ~ *Roger Ascham*

Day: _____ *Date:* ____ / ____ / ____

Today I am *Grateful* for _____

_____

_____

_____

_____

Today's Affirmation _____

Day: _____ *Date:* ____/ ____/ ____

Today I am *Grateful* for _____

_____

_____

_____

_____

_____

Today's Affirmation _____

Love always brings difficulties, that is true, but the good side of it is that it gives energy. ~ *Vincent Van Gogh*

Day: _____ *Date:* ____/ ____/ ____

Today I am *Grateful* for _____

_____

_____

_____

_____

_____

Today's Affirmation _____

Day: _____ *Date:* ____ / ____ / ____

Today I am *Grateful* for _____

_____

_____

_____

_____

Today's Affirmation _____

A thousand words will not leave so deep an impression as one deed.
~ *Henrik Ibsen*

Day: _____ *Date:* ____ / ____ / ____

Today I am *Grateful* for _____

_____

_____

_____

_____

Today's Affirmation _____

Day: _____ *Date:* ____/____/____

Today I am *Grateful* for _____

_____

_____

_____

_____

_____

Today's Affirmation _____

All experience is an arch, to build upon.
~ *Henry Adams*

Day: _____ *Date:* ____/____/____

Today I am *Grateful* for _____

_____

_____

_____

_____

Today's Affirmation _____

Day: _____ *Date:* ____ / ____ / ____

Today I am *Grateful* for _____

_____

_____

_____

_____

Today's Affirmation _____

A thing of beauty is a joy forever: its loveliness increases; it will never pass
into nothingness. ~ *John Keats*

Day: _____ *Date:* ____ / ____ / ____

Today I am *Grateful* for _____

_____

_____

_____

_____

Today's Affirmation _____

Day: _____ *Date:* ____ / ____ / ____

Today I am *Grateful* for _____

_____

_____

_____

_____

_____

Today's Affirmation _____

To have courage for whatever comes in life - everything lies in that.
~ *Saint Teresa of Avila*

Day: _____ *Date:* ____ / ____ / ____

Today I am *Grateful* for _____

_____

_____

_____

_____

_____

Today's Affirmation _____

Day: _____ *Date:* ____ / ____ / ____

Today I am *Grateful* for _____

_____

_____

_____

_____

Today's Affirmation _____

Thank God every morning when you get up that you have something to do
that day, which must be done, whether you like it or not. ~ *James Russell Lowell*

Day: _____ *Date:* ____ / ____ / ____

Today I am *Grateful* for _____

_____

_____

_____

_____

Today's Affirmation _____

Day: _____ *Date:* ____ / ____ / ____

Today I am *Grateful* for _____

_____

_____

_____

_____

Today's Affirmation _____

Gratitude is a duty which ought to be paid, but which none have a
right to expect. ~ *Jean-Jacques Rousseau*

Day: _____ *Date:* ____ / ____ / ____

Today I am *Grateful* for _____

_____

_____

_____

_____

Today's Affirmation _____

Day: _____ *Date:* ____ / ____ / ____

Today I am *Grateful* for _____

_____

_____

_____

_____

Today's Affirmation _____

Little minds are interested in the extraordinary; great minds in the
commonplace. ~ *Elbert Hubbard*

Day: _____ *Date:* ____ / ____ / ____

Today I am *Grateful* for _____

_____

_____

_____

_____

Today's Affirmation _____

Day: _____ *Date:* ____ / ____ / ____

Today I am *Grateful* for _____

_____

_____

_____

_____

_____

Today's Affirmation _____

When you're finished changing, you're finished.
~ *Benjamin Franklin*

Day: _____ *Date:* ____ / ____ / ____

Today I am *Grateful* for _____

_____

_____

_____

_____

_____

Today's Affirmation _____

Day: _____ *Date:* ____/____/____

Today I am *Grateful* for _____

_____

_____

_____

_____

_____

Today's Affirmation _____

Appreciation is a wonderful thing: It makes what is excellent in others
belong to us as well. ~ *Voltaire*

Day: _____ *Date:* ____/____/____

Today I am *Grateful* for _____

_____

_____

_____

_____

_____

Today's Affirmation _____

Day: _____ *Date:* ____ / ____ / ____

Today I am *Grateful* for _____

_____

_____

_____

_____

Today's Affirmation _____

Creativity is not the finding of a thing, but the making something out of it after it is found. ~ *James Russell Lowell*

Day: _____ *Date:* ____ / ____ / ____

Today I am *Grateful* for _____

_____

_____

_____

_____

Today's Affirmation _____

Day: _____ *Date:* ___ / ___ / ___

Today I am *Grateful* for _____

_____

_____

_____

_____

_____

Today's Affirmation _____

> With an eye made quiet by the power of harmony, and the deep
> power of joy, we see into the life of things. ~ *William Wordsworth*

Day: _____ *Date:* ___ / ___ / ___

Today I am *Grateful* for _____

_____

_____

_____

_____

_____

Today's Affirmation _____

Day: _____ *Date:* ____ / ____ / ____

Today I am *Grateful* for _____

_____

_____

_____

_____

_____

Today's Affirmation _____

We consume our tomorrows fretting about our yesterdays. ~ *Persius*

Day: _____ *Date:* ____ / ____ / ____

Today I am *Grateful* for _____

_____

_____

_____

_____

Today's Affirmation _____

Day: _____ *Date:* ____ / ____ / ____

Today I am *Grateful* for _____

_____

_____

_____

_____

_____

Today's Affirmation _____

> You cannot do a kindness too soon, for you never know how soon it
> will be too late. ~ *Ralph Waldo Emerson*

Day: _____ *Date:* ____ / ____ / ____

Today I am *Grateful* for _____

_____

_____

_____

_____

_____

Today's Affirmation _____

Day: _____ *Date:* ____ / ____ / ____

Today I am *Grateful* for _____

_____

_____

_____

_____

_____

Today's Affirmation _____

Genius is the ability to renew one's emotions in daily experience.
~ *Paul Cezanne*

Day: _____ *Date:* ____ / ____ / ____

Today I am *Grateful* for _____

_____

_____

_____

_____

_____

Today's Affirmation _____

Day: _____ *Date:* ____ / ____ / ____

Today I am *Grateful* for _____

_____

_____

_____

_____

_____

Today's Affirmation _____

The measure of a man's real character is what he would do if he knew he
would never be found out. ~ *Thomas Babington Macaulay*

Day: _____ *Date:* ____ / ____ / ____

Today I am *Grateful* for _____

_____

_____

_____

_____

_____

Today's Affirmation _____

Day: _____ *Date:* ____ / ____ / ____

Today I am *Grateful* for _____

_____

_____

_____

_____

_____

Today's Affirmation _____

Begin, be bold and venture to be wise. ~ *Horace*

Day: _____ *Date:* ____ / ____ / ____

Today I am *Grateful* for _____

_____

_____

_____

_____

_____

Today's Affirmation _____

Day: _____ *Date:* ____ / ____ / ____

Today I am *Grateful* for _____

_____

_____

_____

_____

_____

Today's Affirmation _____

I dwell in possibility.
~ Emily Dickinson

Day: _____ *Date:* ____ / ____ / ____

Today I am *Grateful* for _____

_____

_____

_____

_____

Today's Affirmation _____

Day: _____ *Date:* ____ / ____ / ____

Today I am *Grateful* for _____

_____

_____

_____

_____

_____

Today's Affirmation _____

If we learn not humility, we learn nothing. ~ *John Jewel*

Day: _____ *Date:* ____ / ____ / ____

Today I am *Grateful* for _____

_____

_____

_____

_____

_____

Today's Affirmation _____

Day: _____ *Date:* ____/____/____

Today I am *Grateful* for _____

_____

_____

_____

_____

_____

Today's Affirmation _____

If there is no struggle, there is no progress.
~ *Frederick Douglass*

Day: _____ *Date:* ____/____/____

Today I am *Grateful* for _____

_____

_____

_____

_____

Today's Affirmation _____

Day: _____ *Date:* ___/___/___

Today I am *Grateful* for _____

_____

_____

_____

_____

Today's Affirmation _____

The art of being wise is the art of knowing what to overlook.
~ *William James*

Day: _____ *Date:* ___/___/___

Today I am *Grateful* for _____

_____

_____

_____

_____

Today's Affirmation _____

Day: _____ *Date:* ____ / ____ / ____

Today I am *Grateful* for _____

_____

_____

_____

_____

_____

Today's Affirmation _____

Let the beauty of what you love be what you do. ~ *Rumi*

Day: _____ *Date:* ____ / ____ / ____

Today I am *Grateful* for _____

_____

_____

_____

_____

Today's Affirmation _____

Day: _____ *Date:* ____ / ____ / ____

Today I am *Grateful* for _____

_____

_____

_____

_____

Today's Affirmation _____

When I let go of what I am, I become what I might be.
~ *Lao Tzu*

Day: _____ *Date:* ____ / ____ / ____

Today I am *Grateful* for _____

_____

_____

_____

_____

Today's Affirmation _____

Day: _____ *Date:* ____ / ____ / ____

Today I am *Grateful* for _____

_____

_____

_____

_____

Today's Affirmation _____

Seek not to understand that you may believe, but believe that you may
understand. ~ *Saint Augustine*

Day: _____ *Date:* ____ / ____ / ____

Today I am *Grateful* for _____

_____

_____

_____

_____

Today's Affirmation _____

Day: _____ *Date:* ____ / ____ / ____

Today I am *Grateful* for _____

_____

_____

_____

_____

_____

Today's Affirmation _____

Our life is what our thoughts make it. ~ *Marcus Aurelius*

Day: _____ *Date:* ____ / ____ / ____

Today I am *Grateful* for _____

_____

_____

_____

_____

_____

Today's Affirmation _____

Day: _____ Date: ____ / ____ / ____

Today I am *Grateful* for _____

_____

_____

_____

_____

Today's Affirmation _____

They succeed, because they think they can. ~ *Virgil*

Day: _____ Date: ____ / ____ / ____

Today I am *Grateful* for _____

_____

_____

_____

_____

Today's Affirmation _____

Day: _____ *Date:* ____ / ____ / ____

Today I am *Grateful* for _____

_____

_____

_____

_____

_____

Today's Affirmation _____

Success consists of getting up just one more time than you fall.
~ *Oliver Goldsmith*

Day: _____ *Date:* ____ / ____ / ____

Today I am *Grateful* for _____

_____

_____

_____

_____

Today's Affirmation _____

Day: _____ *Date:* ____ / ____ / ____

Today I am *Grateful* for _____

_____

_____

_____

_____

Today's Affirmation _____

Nothing would be done at all if one waited until one could do it so well that
no one could find fault with it. ~ *John Henry Newman*

Day: _____ *Date:* ____ / ____ / ____

Today I am *Grateful* for _____

_____

_____

_____

_____

Today's Affirmation _____

Day: _____ *Date:* ____/____/____

Today I am *Grateful* for _____

_____

_____

_____

_____

Today's Affirmation _____

Good actions give strength to ourselves and inspire good actions in others.
~ *Plato*

Day: _____ *Date:* ____/____/____

Today I am *Grateful* for _____

_____

_____

_____

_____

Today's Affirmation _____

Day: _____ *Date:* ____ / ____ / ____

Today I am *Grateful* for _____

_____

_____

_____

_____

_____

Today's Affirmation _____

Life consists not in holding good cards but in playing those you hold well.
~ *Josh Billings*

Day: _____ *Date:* ____ / ____ / ____

Today I am *Grateful* for _____

_____

_____

_____

_____

_____

Today's Affirmation _____

Day: _____ *Date:* ____ / ____ / ____

Today I am *Grateful* for _____

_____

_____

_____

_____

_____

Today's Affirmation _____

> Do not take life too seriously. You will never get out of it alive.
> ~ *Elbert Hubbard*

Day: _____ *Date:* ____ / ____ / ____

Today I am *Grateful* for _____

_____

_____

_____

_____

_____

Today's Affirmation _____

Day: _____ *Date:* ____ / ____ / ____

Today I am *Grateful* for _____

_____

_____

_____

_____

Today's Affirmation _____

> When unhappy, one doubts everything; when happy, one doubts nothing.
> ~ *Joseph Roux*

Day: _____ *Date:* ____ / ____ / ____

Today I am *Grateful* for _____

_____

_____

_____

_____

Today's Affirmation _____

Day: _____ *Date:* ____ / ____ / ____

Today I am *Grateful* for _____

_____

_____

_____

_____

_____

Today's Affirmation _____

The things that we love tell us what we are. ~ *Thomas Aquinas*

Day: _____ *Date:* ____ / ____ / ____

Today I am *Grateful* for _____

_____

_____

_____

_____

Today's Affirmation _____

Day: _____ *Date:* ____ / ____ / ____

Today I am *Grateful* for _____

_____

_____

_____

_____

Today's Affirmation _____

No man is an island, entire of itself; every man is a piece of the continent.
~ - *John Donne*

Day: _____ *Date:* ____ / ____ / ____

Today I am *Grateful* for _____

_____

_____

_____

_____

Today's Affirmation _____

Day: _____ *Date:* ____/____/____

Today I am *Grateful* for _____

_____

_____

_____

_____

Today's Affirmation _____

Friends are the sunshine of life. ~ *John Hay*

Day: _____ *Date:* ____/____/____

Today I am *Grateful* for _____

_____

_____

_____

_____

Today's Affirmation _____

Day: _____ *Date:* ____ / ____ / ____

Today I am *Grateful* for _____

_____

_____

_____

_____

_____

Today's Affirmation _____

There is nothing like a dream to create the future. ~ *Victor Hugo*

Day: _____ *Date:* ____ / ____ / ____

Today I am *Grateful* for _____

_____

_____

_____

_____

_____

Today's Affirmation _____

Day: _____ *Date:* ____ / ____ / ____

Today I am *Grateful* for _____

_____

_____

_____

_____

_____

Today's Affirmation _____

The strongest principle of growth lies in the human choice.
~ *George Eliot*

Day: _____ *Date:* ____ / ____ / ____

Today I am *Grateful* for _____

_____

_____

_____

_____

_____

Today's Affirmation _____

Day: _____ *Date:* ____ / ____ / ____

Today I am *Grateful* for _____

_____

_____

_____

_____

_____

Today's Affirmation _____

Absence sharpens love, presence strengthens it. ~ *Thomas Fuller*

Day: _____ *Date:* ____ / ____ / ____

Today I am *Grateful* for _____

_____

_____

_____

_____

_____

Today's Affirmation _____

Day: _____ *Date:* ____/ ____/ ____

Today I am *Grateful* for _____

_____

_____

_____

_____

_____

Today's Affirmation _____

What worries you, masters you. ~ *John Locke*

Day: _____ *Date:* ____/ ____/ ____

Today I am *Grateful* for _____

_____

_____

_____

_____

Today's Affirmation _____

Day: _____ *Date:* ____ / ____ / ____

Today I am *Grateful* for _____

_____

_____

_____

_____

_____

Today's Affirmation _____

Events will take their course, it is no good of being angry at them; he is
happiest who wisely turns them to the best account. ~ *Euripides*

Day: _____ *Date:* ____ / ____ / ____

Today I am *Grateful* for _____

_____

_____

_____

_____

_____

Today's Affirmation _____

Day: _____ *Date:* ____ / ____ / ____

Today I am *Grateful* for _____

_____

_____

_____

_____

Today's Affirmation _____

Truly, it is in darkness that one finds the light, so when we are in sorrow, then
this light is nearest of all to us. ~ *Meister Eckhart*

Day: _____ *Date:* ____ / ____ / ____

Today I am *Grateful* for _____

_____

_____

_____

_____

Today's Affirmation _____

Day: _____ *Date:* ____ / ____ / ____

Today I am *Grateful* for _____

_____

_____

_____

_____

_____

Today's Affirmation _____

Nothing will ever be attempted if all possible objections must
first be overcome. ~ *Samuel Johnson*

Day: _____ *Date:* ____ / ____ / ____

Today I am *Grateful* for _____

_____

_____

_____

_____

_____

Today's Affirmation _____

Day: _____ *Date:* ____/____/____

Today I am *Grateful* for _____

_____

_____

_____

_____

_____

Today's Affirmation _____

You must accept the truth from whatever source it comes.
~ Maimonides

Day: _____ *Date:* ____/____/____

Today I am *Grateful* for _____

_____

_____

_____

_____

_____

Today's Affirmation _____

Day: _____ *Date:* ____ / ____ / ____

Today I am *Grateful* for _____

_____

_____

_____

_____

_____

Today's Affirmation _____

Our opportunities to do good are our talents. ~ *Cotton Mather*

Day: _____ *Date:* ____ / ____ / ____

Today I am *Grateful* for _____

_____

_____

_____

_____

Today's Affirmation _____

Day: _____ *Date:* ____/____/____

Today I am *Grateful* for _____

_____

_____

_____

_____

_____

Today's Affirmation _____

Either I will find a way, or I will make one. ~ *Philip Sidney*

Day: _____ *Date:* ____/____/____

Today I am *Grateful* for _____

_____

_____

_____

_____

_____

Today's Affirmation _____

Day: _____ *Date:* ____/____/____

Today I am *Grateful* for _____

_____

_____

_____

_____

_____

Today's Affirmation _____

We love life, not because we are used to living but because we are
used to loving. ~ *Friedrich Nietzsche*

Day: _____ *Date:* ____/____/____

Today I am *Grateful* for _____

_____

_____

_____

_____

Today's Affirmation _____

Day: _____ *Date:* ____ / ____ / ____

Today I am *Grateful* for _____

_____

_____

_____

_____

_____

Today's Affirmation _____

If you wished to be loved, love. ~ *Lucius Annaeus Seneca*

Day: _____ *Date:* ____ / ____ / ____

Today I am *Grateful* for _____

_____

_____

_____

_____

_____

Today's Affirmation _____

Day: _____ *Date:* ____ / ____ / ____

Today I am *Grateful* for _____

_____

_____

_____

_____

_____

Today's Affirmation _____

It does not matter how slowly you go as long as you do not stop.
~ *Confucius*

Day: _____ *Date:* ____ / ____ / ____

Today I am *Grateful* for _____

_____

_____

_____

_____

_____

Today's Affirmation _____

Day: _____ *Date:* ____/ ____/ ____

Today I am *Grateful* for _____

_____

_____

_____

_____

_____

Today's Affirmation _____

Love has reasons which reason cannot understand.
~ *Blaise Pascal*

Day: _____ *Date:* ____/ ____/ ____

Today I am *Grateful* for _____

_____

_____

_____

_____

_____

Today's Affirmation _____

Day: _____ *Date:* ____ / ____ / ____

Today I am *Grateful* for _____

_____

_____

_____

_____

_____

Today's Affirmation _____

We are here to add what we can to life, not to get what we can from life.
~ *William Osler*

Day: _____ *Date:* ____ / ____ / ____

Today I am *Grateful* for _____

_____

_____

_____

_____

_____

Today's Affirmation _____

Day: _____ *Date:* ____/ ____/ ____

Today I am *Grateful* for _____

_____

_____

_____

_____

_____

Today's Affirmation _____

True knowledge exists in knowing that you know nothing. ~ *Socrates*

Day: _____ *Date:* ____/ ____/ ____

Today I am *Grateful* for _____

_____

_____

_____

_____

_____

Today's Affirmation _____

Day: _____ *Date:* ____/ ____/ ____

Today I am *Grateful* for _____

_____

_____

_____

_____

Today's Affirmation _____

It's not what happens to you, but how you react to it that matters.
~ *Epictetus*

Day: _____ *Date:* ____/ ____/ ____

Today I am *Grateful* for _____

_____

_____

_____

_____

Today's Affirmation _____

Day: _____ *Date:* ____ / ____ / ____

Today I am *Grateful* for _____

_____

_____

_____

_____

_____

Today's Affirmation _____

Fortune favors the bold. ~ *Virgil*

Day: _____ *Date:* ____ / ____ / ____

Today I am *Grateful* for _____

_____

_____

_____

_____

Today's Affirmation _____

Day: _____ *Date:* ____ / ____ / ____

Today I am *Grateful* for _____

_____

_____

_____

_____

Today's Affirmation _____

> That which does not kill us makes us stronger.
> ~ *Friedrich Nietzsche*

Day: _____ *Date:* ____ / ____ / ____

Today I am *Grateful* for _____

_____

_____

_____

_____

Today's Affirmation _____

Day: _____ *Date:* ____ / ____ / ____

Today I am *Grateful* for _____

_____

_____

_____

_____

Today's Affirmation _____

As people are walking all the time, in the same spot, a path appears.
~ *John Locke*

Day: _____ *Date:* ____ / ____ / ____

Today I am *Grateful* for _____

_____

_____

_____

_____

Today's Affirmation _____

Made in the USA
Monee, IL
06 November 2022

17249567R00066